World Cultures

Jo Chambers

Contents

Culture and Customs

The world is a huge place, full of different people with different customs, traditions, and ways of life.

This book explores some cultures, past and present. Where do you think the people in these photos live? Are they from the past or the present?

How many are wearing hats or headdresses?

These children are at school. Is the classroom different from yours? How?

There are 7 rows of 2 desks in a classroom. How many desks are there altogether?

Aztecs

The Aztec people lived more than 500 years ago in Mexico.

The royal palaces were in the middle of the cities. The ruler and his household lived upstairs, and government officials lived downstairs.

Are there more people upstairs or downstairs?

Are there more rooms upstairs or downstairs? How many rooms are there altogether?

Aztecs traded goods with each other in huge markets. How many of each item is shown in the picture?

Like us, the Aztecs used symbols to represent different numbers. Unlike us, they used pictures for writing.

Key

● = 1

⚑ = 20

Honey jar

Blankets

Shields

The Maya and Inca

About 2,000 years ago, the Maya lived in what is now Mexico and Central America. They used dots and bars for writing numbers in their math system.

These are the symbols for the number 12. What could the dots and bars stand for?

Here is an addition number sentence. What numbers have been added? Can you figure out the total?

Write your age using the Mayan system.

KEY WORDS

- addition
- total
- ones
- fives
- tens

The Inca lived in what is now South America about 500 years ago. Their empire had more than 12 million people.

Archeologists have discovered how the Inca recorded numbers. This is called a "quipu." It shows 2 pieces of string with knots in them.

This quipu shows the number 23. Can you see how it works?

You can use string and knots to make your own quipu. What would your age look like?

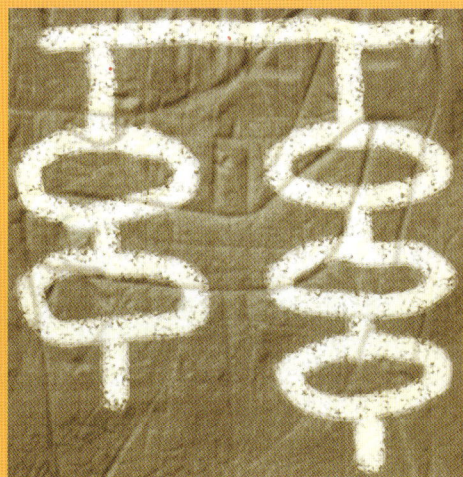

How could a quipu show a 3-digit number?

Ancient Egyptians

The ancient Egyptians believed in life after death. So when a person died, the body was mummified to preserve it for the next life.

The mummy was often buried inside a coffin in a tomb. Tombs also held things a person might need in the next life, such as food, money, and weapons.

How many gold items can you see?
What if half of them were stolen?
How many would be left?

KEY WORDS
- how many?
- half
- total
- double
- triple

FACT! Tutankhamen's tomb was opened in 1922 and was full of treasures.

Like the Aztecs, the Egyptians used pictures to write. The pictures are called "hieroglyphs." How many cows would there be if the size of the herd doubled? Tripled?

List how many of each color cow there would be if the number doubled.

1	2	3	4	5	6	7
8	9	10	11	12	13	14
15	16	17	18	19	20	21

Ancient Greeks

The ancient Greeks built theaters more than 2,000 years ago. All the actors were men who wore masks and costumes.

Stone tokens were used as tickets with seat numbers. Are these 2 seats next to each other? This pair of tokens happen to add up to 10.

Are there other pairs of tickets that add up to 10? Will any of these people be able to sit next to each other?

Pythagoras was a famous Greek mathematician. He explored the shapes that could be made from different numbers of stones.

KEY WORDS

- add
- next to
- order
- how many?

Get 25 counters. Find out which numbers from 1 to 25 can be arranged to make triangles and which can be arranged to make squares.

Make a list of the triangle numbers less than 30. How many counters have been added each time to make the next triangle number?

TOOLS

1	2	3	4	5	6	7	8	9	10
11	12	13	14	15	16	17	18	19	20
21	22	23	24	25	26	27	28	29	30

Romans

More than 3,000 years ago, a group of settlers lived on the hills where Rome is today. They became known as Romans.

Romans loved chariot racing. Teams of drivers and chariots pulled by 4 horses would race around an oval track. Many horses and drivers would crash.

How many horses are still racing? How many have fallen? Figure out the total.

If there are 20 horses are in the race, how many chariots are there?

The Romans had a strong army. When attacking, they grouped into a rectangular block with shields around and above them. This was called a *testudo*, or tortoise.

There are 5 rows of 4 soldiers each in this testudo. How many soldiers are there? You can add or multiply to find the answer.

Show different testudo groups for 12 soldiers.

Could you have a testudo with 11 soldiers?

Maasai from Africa

The Maasai are a group of people from Kenya and Tanzania in eastern Africa. They are livestock herders who move with their cattle every dry season to find new grass.

Their homes are arranged in groups. If there are 5 groups of 3 homes in this circle, how many homes are there in total?

Find different ways to arrange 5 groups of 3 homes.

The Maasai love singing and playing games in their spare time. How many more women need to join this group to make 15 altogether?

KEY WORDS

- multiply
- total
- arrange
- altogether
- make

This game is called "*bao.*" Two players move seeds around a board, trying to capture the other player's seeds.

How many brown seeds are there? How many yellow seeds are there? How many more of each are needed to make 15?

TOOLS

1 2 3 4 5 6 7 8 9 10

Desert Dwellers

The Tuareg are nomadic people from the Sahara Desert. They travel across the desert with their animals, looking for grazing land.

How many camels are in this camel train? How many more are needed to make 20?

The Sahara is hot and dry in the day but cold at night. The Tuareg carry tents with them to sleep in at night.

In the Sahara Desert, the temperature can rise to more than 120°F (50°C).

FACT!

If each tent can sleep 2 people, how many will the group need?

The San have lived in the Kalahari Desert for 20,000 years. In the past, they were hunter-gatherers.

The women collected nuts and berries and dug for roots. The men went out in groups to hunt animals. How many women are there? How many men and women?

Hunters follow animal tracks. They can tell from the tracks if an animal is wounded.

The 2 people with bows have 20 arrows between them. How many arrows could each have?

TOOLS

1	2	3	4	5	6	7	8	9	10
11	12	13	14	15	16	17	18	19	20

17

Inuit of the Arctic

It can be -40°F (-40°C) in the Arctic. These Inuit are dressed to stay warm. How many boots can you see? How many more would make 12?

In the Arctic, winter is dark for most of the day and night. When the summer begins, there are festivals to celebrate.

If there are 5 people on each side of the blanket, how many are there altogether?

Snowmobiles are used to travel across the ice and snow.

This snowmobile can hold 10 people. How many more people can travel in it?

FACT!

In temperatures below freezing, the Inuit may build a snow shelter called a "quinzhee."

There are 4 snowmobiles carrying 6 people each. How many are riding in the snowmobiles?

TOOLS

1	2	5	6	9	10	13	14	17	18	21	22
3	4	7	8	11	12	15	16	19	20	23	24

Mountain People

Sherpas mainly live in the northeastern Himalayas in Nepal. Since the 1950s, they have taken part in expeditions to climb Mount Everest.

FACT!

Mount Everest is more than 29,000 feet (8,800 m) tall!

If each Sherpa carries a 20 pound (9 kg) pack, how much will they carry altogether?

Before each climb up Mount Everest, the Sherpas and other climbers say prayers in a "Puja" ceremony.

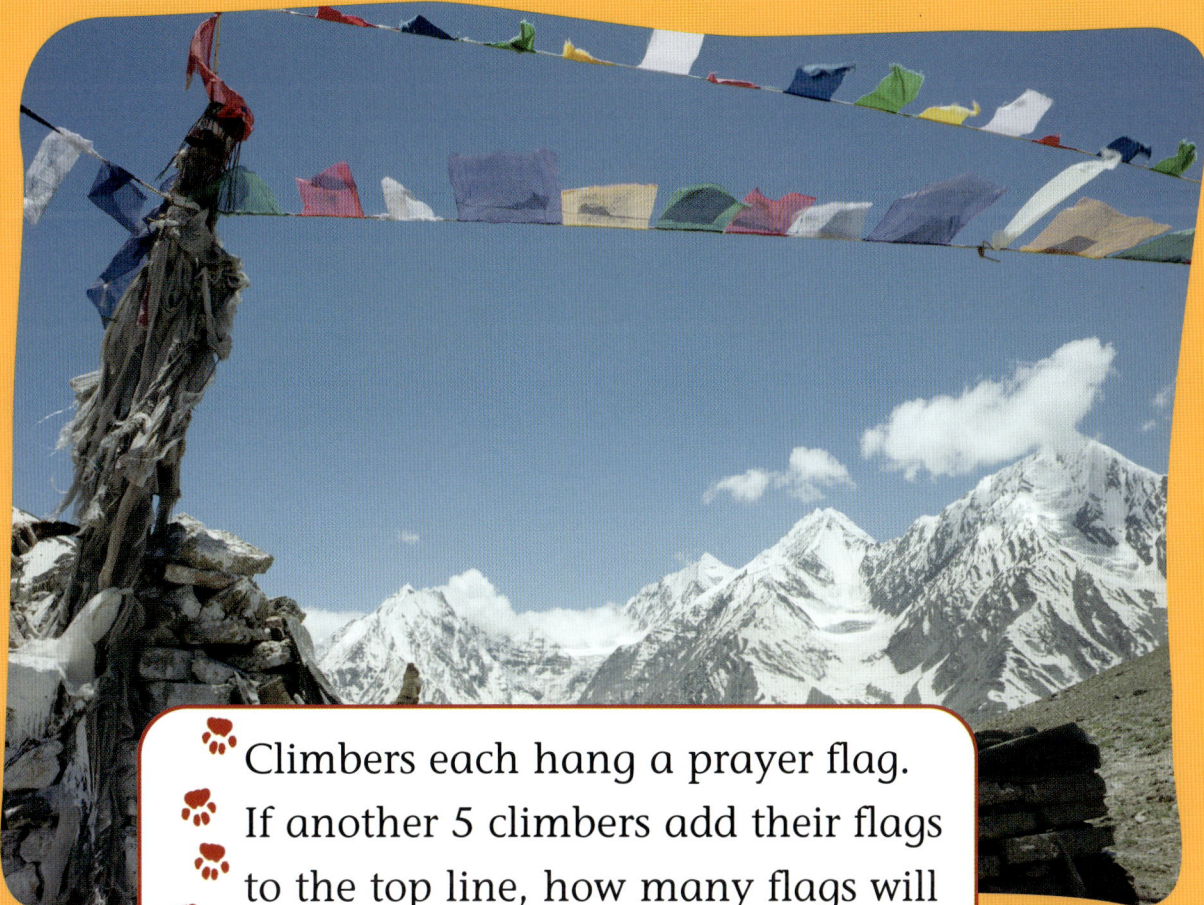

Climbers each hang a prayer flag. If another 5 climbers add their flags to the top line, how many flags will there be in that line?

Figure out the total number of flags, including the 5 new ones.

TOOLS

| 0 | 10 | 20 | 30 | 40 | 50 | 60 | 70 | 80 | 90 | 100 |

Maoris of New Zealand

The first people to settle in New Zealand were the Maoris.

The traditional Maori meeting house is often decorated with *kowhaiwhai* patterns. These are made by sliding, flipping, and turning a shape called a *"koru."*

FACT!

The Maoris came from central Polynesia about 800 years ago.

How many rows of *korus* can you see? Imagine 3 meeting houses with this pattern. How many *korus* would there be altogether?

The *haka* is a traditional Maori war dance. It is also performed by the New Zealand rugby team, the All Blacks, at the start of a game.

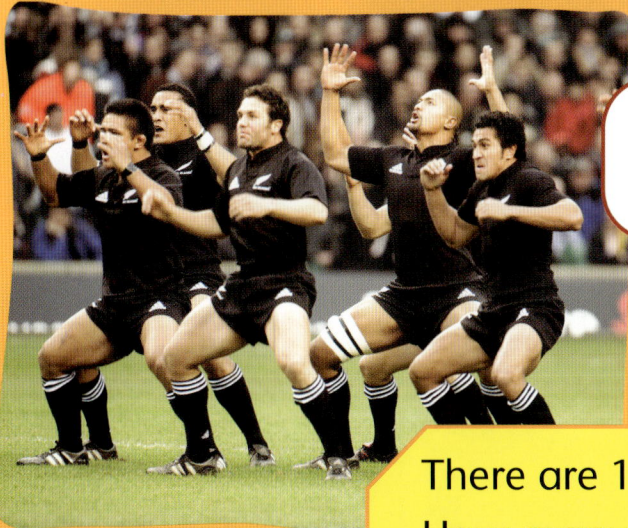

Figure out the total number of people doing the *haka*.

There are 15 people on a rugby team. How many more need to be added here to make a complete team?

TOOLS

1	2	3	4	5	6	7	8	9	10
11	12	13	14	15	16	17	18	19	20

Sum It Up

Find the total for this problem using Mayan numbers.

3 **8**

$$\text{OO} + \text{OOO} =$$

6 **4**

Which pairs of digit cards make 10?
Write down other pairs that make 10.

9 **2**   **7** **3**   **5** **6**

Each person catches 3 fish. How many do they catch altogether?